# Second Coming/
# *Return of the Herd*

Lobibah Oji Baraka
(Gilbert H. Richards)

Second Coming | Return of the Herd

© 2023, Gilbert H. Richards

First Edition, 2024

# Dedications

To my sister, Adina Carter, whose presence and support always nagged but nurtured me. I am humbled and remorseful.

To my spiritual adviser, Ms. Ethel S. Linney, who thought of me as more than a patron but a friend and advocate.

To Mildred E. Faulkner and Linda J. Alexander, whose friendships I will always treasure.

# Acknowledgments

To **Matthew Lippman** of Gotham Writers, my mentor and guru, who encouraged and inspired me to produce and share my works.

To **Anne Marie Wells** of Community Literature Initiative (CLI), whose passion, charisma, knowledge and expertise motivated and guided me in refining and selecting poems for this book.

And much love to my DMV chapter, Season 10 classmates, who provided consciousness and context for my poems.

# Contents

# Preface

In his book *SECOND COMING/Return of the Herd*, poet Lobibah Oji Baraka (Gilbert H. Richards) continues his compelling journey through socio-political and nostalgic spheres with artistic intellect and resonant energy. His poetry has been described as layered, textured, provocative, sensual, reflective, and commemorative.

His persona speaks with an attitude that is genuine and a vibe that is ripe. Sometimes fuming, other times funky—but always intriguing and relatable.

The book is divided into five sections: Self, arts, death, love and society.

Baraka writes with a flair for the narrative. His poems possess verbal sophistication that has been described as "sonic deliciousness." His figurative language is "visually compelling."

Baraka's latest edition is a culmination of authentic free verse as well as compelling, reflective prose poetry.

# Section One

*Let him speak who has seen with his eyes.*

**-Congolese proverb**

# Momma Was Right

"Gilbert" – That's what my momma named me.
Strong American name, she says.
Maybe for a stuffy white guy.
Illustrious and distinguished—
I looked the name up, okay?
I own it because those were her aspirations
for me.  I hold homage to her, shouldering
onus like an atlas.

So, why not "Albert" like my Daddy? He named the girls,
she the boys. But you named me "Heliobus" after him?
She gave me a look, so I looked
elsewhere but couldn't find nothing. Except "Helios"—the Greek
Sun-god with his four-horse sky-chariot.
Hmm, "Sun-rider" was my translation.

Let me re-introduce MYSELF: Daddy's Heliobus became Me–
"Loby," and then the poet-writer, "Lobibah."

The late '70s blasted off with quasi-afro names.
The sonic fix was in, spiced and spliced with sha and shi's,
ra and ri's, na and ni's, da and de's,
ma-my's, cha-chi's and ja-je's.

Oh my, even me, "the gift-bearer."
In Swahili—I am Oji.

Yet also, the prophet who sees and knows more
truths than he speaks. I am clarion for
the Diaspora,  leader for the wayward
and welcome for the lost.
I am root for harvest and voice for visions.

I understand now. Momma was right.
Lobibah Oji Baraka—that's me.

## You Oughta Know

If I don't get it right in life,
 ever get it right I ain't
worried bout it.
I'm all right.

If I don't ever marry again,
don't ever have children—
know this: I'm all right,
Ain't much gonna fight it.

Destiny or fate comes late enough as is:
All right. Live and let live!
I yam what I yam, and that's all!

Take or leave it, reject, receive
 or straight believe it. Jus know
I ain't much worried bout it!

Not to say I haven't learned

some things. Every day above ground

is a good day, a lesson.

And the peace of mind's a blessing,

A treasure – priceless.

My God is awesome!


But I got enuff stuff spinning

roun my head that I gotta sort.

Enuff trials to figure out.

So pardon me if I don't shout.

I ain't much worried.

Ain't got time.


Do you mind

me being all right?

## **Seed Season**

I am a seed
upon the ground
Alone
Out of season

A bead of spit
I am
 in need
My pulse needs rest
My heart needs a refuge

Where do I turn from the cold?
the heat, the dark, the day?
I've learned to expect
No less
than time and space
A season

Do I need luck for shelter?

Or shelter for luck?

Is love luck?

Really?

How much

do I want or need?

How much

can I?

Is that happiness?

Is that success?


Or is it me?

Should I believe in love's nutrients

and nuances to the nth?


Save me; who wants to try?

I am naked and blind.

Who can open my eyes and cleanse my lenses?

Be my knees, arms, my hands, feet--

Caress and nurture me?

Sure, I need bones and  tongue too

No less

A mess am I


Love? I've seen it darken

and ignite, trigger and explode,

fight and flee
Wrong and right
Folks kill and die for it and
Kill and die without it
I'm senseless

God of Mercy, take root
Lead me, guide me, rescue me
Destiny is
my dilemma, my salvation

Heavenly Father, though I'm spit,
Bless me anyway
in my season

# Wet

I'm a city guy who likes water

but not being in it or on it.

Yeah, I like playing with cool and wet memories.

Swimming in chlorinated pools, wading,

dog-paddling, stroking and diving.


I like spraying with rubber hoses, fire hydrants and lawn sprinklers.

Gulping from kitchen spigots, park fountains and pitchers

filled with ice cubes.

Ahh! Belching is beautiful.

I like the steam of warm showers and soaking

in four-pawed porcelain bathtubs.


I'm no beach bum or rustic, but I like watching water too.

Peaceful ponds, stirring streams and foamy shores.

Nostalgia brings ripples of tranquility— indeed refreshing,

a cathartic thirst.

Yet two or three hours of therapy is enough.

Can't wait to see the city.

## Work

Sometimes I stack 'whys' and 'what-ifs.'

like alphabet blocks. Other times

I weigh worries on sinking and rising scales.

Then again, my positions shift like bike pedals.

I'm in constant limbo.


What happened to the presents of promise?

The white-collar jobs and prominent academies?

If not for the spin of dead ends, what

could have been? And even so, with whom

would I share the spoils? There's only


Me: a single short-rooted tree—

two limbed with branches a few.

No seeds, no fruit. Only me.

What type of father would I've been?

Would this have changed me? Would I've been

Teddy bear, pit bull, mule or ass?

Or all four and more?

Guess things turn the way they're supposed to.

A life enhanced by flesh and flavors

spread and sampled among tricks and trials.


No matter how altered the pursuits, there remain

keys to turn and locks to open. Still searching.


Enough! I've much work to do.

## Bye, Miss Bradley (4th Q Blues)

"What does my son gotta do to pass?"

Well, first—I smirk—he must listen and pay attention.

He chooses not to.

"Can he make it up?"

Not really. It's the fourth quarter. 10 months have gone already.

"Guess he gotta do summer school then."

Perhaps. But I'm so disappointed, Mom. He's certainly capable.

"I know; that boy makes me so mad sometimes."

Really, I just want effort and engagement.

Figure the two actions will produce measurable achievement.

"Said he rather do summer school."

 We understood.

Nevertheless, I'm still his best bet for passing.

"Yep, I'll get him ready for next year, Mr. Richards."

I'm counting on it. Bye, Miss Bradley.

*Summer school's a 3-week credit scam for 10 months of stank.*

# Message From Stuttering Stan

Smart alecks like to test teachers. Like hecklers,

their agenda is to disrupt and distort.

Disrupt the instruction and distort the message.

I had enough of this one opportunistic, attention-snatching hawk.

He likes to flaunt his taunts.

"How you gonna teach English

when you can't even talk?"

"Same as any other English teacher?

Why do you think differently?"

He claims that he doesn't understand

what I say; I don't talk right.

"Okay, but everybody else understands– you sure

the problem, isn't you?"

"It ain't me; I don't stutter."


He doesn't understand my directions and expectations;

pretends not to understand anything I say.

I pause, gazing at his smug goofiness.

"So young fella, what does that have to do with teaching English?

You know we're talking about two different things, right?"

I know by now he's lost interest in me–

his feeble humor has expired.

Nonetheless, I jab him, stab him with teacher qualifications,

degrees, certifications, tenures and evaluations.


He is ready to move on. But I'm not ready to free him.

I resume my gamesmanship, angling him toward the corner

of Writing & Mechanics.

Then hooking him with body shots of genres

until he slumps to the floor. The bell rings.


He's a little wobbly, but I think he gets it: Teaching

isn't just lecturing, giving directions and managing the class.

It's about learning and understanding what's being taught.


"Any more questions? Enough explanations!

Let's get back to work, my man. You owe me

some work, don't you? And I'm going

to hold you to it."

## Color Tv

Mostly everyone– except my household–

had color TVs – the "It things" in 1966.

Some neighborhood folkz had a notion to "colorize" their consoles.

They scotch-taped a 3- colored screen of pale blue, light pink

and green crepe over gray images.


At 9 years old, I understood their agenda

but not their method.

To me, shades of blue are shades of blue—

not colors.

And I was right! The landscape was okay,

but the striped people looked weird.


Then my stylish Aunt Teen bought a new "It set"

— and everything was "go"!

The crosstown bus ride didn't matter.

 I got an ark-load of animated duos to see,

like Bugs & Daffy, Rocky & Bullwinkle,

Tom & Jerry.

The Flintstones & Jetsons were family sitcoms

like Lucy & Desi and Dick & Mary.


When I hear a Rascally Rabbit's "What's up, Doc?"

Or the smallest caped powerhouse roar,

"Here I come to save the day!"

Or a portly caveman cheer.

I'm in Saturday morning glory.


55+ years later, the experience smiles on me still.

"Yabba dabba doo!"

## Fruit Bowl

I'm no world traveler, no ocean cruiser, roadrunner

or cross-country courier.

 I'm a "staycationer."


A space and place at home is all I need to relax—

a thinking square to ruminate on life,

and a reflection sphere—to sort and sequence

matters of mind and body.


But when I'm feeling good, I mean really good –
Cool dessert is my go-to!


I walk to the corner cabinet, turn on the sports radio,

thumb the T.V. remote, and secure the premises.
Clamping down on my sofa, I settle into a scene.


Then I go to the refrigerator and get my favorite.

Fruit bowl makes me roll over like a tickled puppy!


Chunks of green grapes, oranges, melons, pineapples

and cantaloupes rope me hostage.

I bite into a mesh of succulent flavors,

ingesting scrumptious tropical colors-- and smile

as if I were in Montego Bay or St. Thomas.


That's as close as I care to get to the Caribbean.

Chillin is a feelin. Fruit bowl time!

# Altar Of Hand
# Part 1


My big right hand, with its thick fingers, wasn't always so.

Once, my little righty grasped crayons and pencils that looped

lines into ovals and angles, morphing and connecting static rhythms

into messages of fantasy and affirmation.

Free thoughts are signified and endorsed.


My adolescent righty summoned the artist in me to awaken.

I presided over linear ascents, graphic accents,

unwrapped notions into likenesses, colors into worlds.


There settled, in my teen hand, a joy harnessed,

a power to seal and sustain, release and reveal.

There, an impulse humbled my focus and fired my senses.

I knelt at my sanctum-- Altar of the Hand.


My young man hand expressed life as spectra and graphite,

puzzles and promises, heavens and horrors.

My fingers, active levers and transformative gears, delivered hues on pads and canvases of midnights and dawns.

My eyes explored orbits of reality, translating sight

into thoughts and thoughts into things

and words into substance.


I graduated from college.

The world summoned, and I surrendered.

Bachelor's degree without destination.

I left the Altar.

## Altar Of Hand
## Part 2

For an aspiring artist or nascent novice, a wish

is a dream ashore. I chose the required

responsibilities of adulthood: paydays.


Then a Voice beyond spoke to me—a middle-aged man.

I remembered, as a child, feeling its presence

but not knowing its name.


As a young man, I recalled turning away, leaving

the Altar. I abandoned my pledge, choosing survival, choosing life.

I sketched less and celebrated more—

on basketball courts and in nightclubs. I wandered,

losing ignition for the arts.


That Voice forced me to recall my purpose.

The ultimate—of my own hand—

and its magnitude as a doer, performer,

give-and-taker, make-and-breaker,

and hold-folder.

For years I yearned to regain it, reclaim

that power to manifest, even magnify it.


That night, I knelt before the Altar.

My golden right hand radiated! I was alive

—reborn. A wonder surged through my palm

and pulsated through my fingers.


I am

a child of discovery

—a vessel of verve.

# Waiting On The Lab

Perching on the ledge of a black sofa, I nestle
bare feet into bluish gray carpet.
Upon my right leg rests a blank sheet like an easel.
Holding my ink pen like a brush–I wait.
I settle into my lab, my creative shelter.

On the wall, glass art of Zulu silhouettes with spears and shields
waits. We focus on the signal—the drum of inspiration.
I prepare for an encounter with the Muse.

On the shelf across the room, I see figurines of panthers
prowling and elephants curling trunks
to tongues of tom-toms.
Yet the Sankofa bird carries eggs of promise.
Looking to the past for insight.
Looking to the present for reflection.
 But exploring tomorrow for inspiration.

On the top shelf, I survey familial images.
Where my roots rise into stalks and leaves:
Granma, Ma and my siblings.

Then from the third shelf, a man, robed in red, steps forward.

Past the long-tusked elephant and black drinking gourd,

holding in his right arm, the tom-tom.

He lifts his left hand and pounds primal chants into sonic codes.

 I listen to ancestral choruses.
I close my eyes, waiting for engagement—
and smile.

# That Spirit Thing

A silver arrow necklace from Avon Cosmetics.
That's the accessory I remember in high school.
The warrior spirit– I felt it. Not just a trend
but a symbol. More than an accent
but an axis of identity.

My '73 Morgan State brethren from the Motherland
greeted me, mistaking me as them. They awaited
acknowledgment and grew disenchanted because
I never conversed. Not knowing them, I only nodded.
Then one afternoon, one brotha greeted me and
offered a gift—a necklace. Surprised
and humbled, I accepted and thanked him.

He asked of my ethnicity—African state or Caribbean Isle?
Neither-- I'm an East Baltimore native.
Dark brown with a broad forehead,
high cheekbones, wide nose, and full lips.
In Nigeria, he claimed, I would be Ife and Benin royalty.
I liked the idea and loved the concept of continental kinship.

I never considered myself "cool." The casual, conservative
and "pedestrian" could describe me. I considered fashionistas
too busy, too expensive, too outlandish, too slick.
Yet in the early '70s, I spent summers in Brooklyn, NY,

having a blast and spreading my "hip" wings.
I sported wide brims, butterfly collars, double-knit flairs,
platform shoes, cotton and rayons in prints
of whites, lights, and louds.

Not to mention cologne. But for me—no gaudy gold
and diamond-studded ropes with initials and icons.
For me, gold and silver-painted necklaces connected.
Especially if they reflected the African warrior.

40 years later, I still favor "That Afrika thing, not the bling."
I can go casual or cultural. Just a thang. I can sport
a necklace with large tan and yellow wooden beads.
Or the Africa piece with red, black and green.
Or the wooden "God is Supreme" emblem outlined in gold.

My swagger. My thang! Yet I can level up
when I want—with necklaces of black opal
or epic flower medallion.
Or black elephants and tassels with turquoise mini-beads.
Or my pride 'n joy necklace of opal beads and stones, with lion
and elephant totem carvings.

Been a minute since the Morgan "bling,"
and I still can't shake that thing.

## Jesus Loves Me, 2022

"Yes, Jesus loves me, 'cause the Bible tells
me so," I sang as a child in Sunday School.
"We are weak, but he is strong."

Yes, the Bible told me, but I didn't know
Jesus. Not really know about his heritage
 and ministry then. You see, I wasn't raised
Baptist, but a nighthawk and working stump
– a bachelor at 33. I couldn't understand
Jesus until I was baptized.

'A wet devil,' my Aunt Teen would remark.
She meant a 'soaked sinner.' As a Christian
I've been doused aplenty. I'm no different than
any other man though he may speak of race,
family, work and class, purpose
and ambition, hope and prayer.

I've learned a little something about Jesus,
his teachings of faith and repentance.
His commitment to commandments and gospels.

I've learned more about myself. I know

I'm a sinner. A seed and beam, a symbol

and psalm. A blossom.

I'm fruit of the Spirit. A love

that blankets and blesses. A joy that leaps

and weeps. A peace that powders and perfumes.

A goodness that nurtures and gardens.

A gentleness jeweled. A kindness crowned.

A faithfulness fueled. A patience empowered.

A self-control sanctified.


At 67, I learned –at Elder Elementary Bible School – the depths

of baptism in streams of Babylon.

My soul is refreshed and, yes, nourished.


And oh, the Bible tells me about a Nazarene carpenter and healer

who gives the weary and weak rest and willpower, who ushers joy

to the afflicted and brokenhearted, and liberty

to the downtrodden and damned.


The Bible tells me of a rabbi who anoints and announces recovery

and favor. It tells me to listen to a prophet who arises from

and encourages repentance of and confesses compassion

for the people.

Despite me and in spite of the world, the Bible tells me about a Messiah whose Gauntlet is the Gospel.

That's why I know

Jesus loves me much.

## Majesty Of Nostalgia

If you could throw, you threw. If you could run,
chase and tag, you did.
Rules were simple and few; all you had to do
was do. Laughter rang, long and loud. Play
was play—no gray area—no pain, no grimacing.
No slapping or smacking. No hurt, no foul.

Anything with a ball trumped all. Throw and catch, dodgeball,
"it" ball, block ball, step ball, curb ball and 3 flies.
No lie! Did I say we had "fun" back in 1960s Baltimore?

When we didn't chase and race, we rolled
battery-operated toy cars, trucks and trains from our knees and
scraped elbows on wagons and bikes.
We jumped alleys and steps and climbed fences and walls.
We played outdoors and only stopped for lunch breaks and supper.

Parents didn't have to tell us about Play 60.
Play was unofficial and rarely organized, and never sanctioned.
It was a neighborhood standard of Whosoever Will.
Just choose a team—Who's next?
Onlookers gathered for entertainment.
No matter the selection, the competition was equal.
The top guys were top guys in all sports.

Instead of ball play, kids in the 2000s tinker and toggle
on gadgets and vie for supremacy on virtual games.
Eyes blink, fingers and thumbs twitch as remotes twist.
On electric scooters and skateboards, they glide.
This is how they used their powers, speed and agility—to fly.
Not us. We flexed our "muscles" in GTOs, Mustangs, Firebirds
and Malibu's.
No hybrid and plug-and-play rides.

We experienced the taste of what we ate and drank,
the touch of what we felt, the belief of what
we saw and the decibels of what we heard.
No illusions or projected fantasies, no CGI
or IMAX for us. Virtual nothing!

Being there is the thing – the prize.
The Wonder of Whatever, Wherever
and Whenever makes nostalgia
electric, even majestic.

## Rolling In Riches

"I've been rich," once said Pearl Bailey,
"and I've been poor. I like rich a whole lot better."
Guess I've always been a lil better than "po."
Maybe "at-risk" or "low-income." Just didn't know
how much because it didn't matter.
Everyone around me was like me.

I was always folding dollars in my pockets
and dropping coins in a piggy bank.
"Survival," I called it.
How economical the practical.
If a man couldn't take of himself, what good was he?
Money was means to an end–an enemy or friend.
Just a dimension of reality.

Earning enough was cool. Calculating and budgeting
were my scales. Income inked my social and professional
thermometer. Life for me had always been a lane
of routine jobs until I shifted to a faster career curve.
My grind shined.
I saw the sunrise of education and knew where to go: teaching
literature and composition. Yet not quite know how to get there
—if ever.
I saw the light: I knew I could write.

Benefits and health insurance aligned
with my visions and enhanced my efforts.
I saw sun rising horizons. I watched and waited for sunsets.
I counted coins for utilities and doled out dollars for leisure.

It took a minute, some decades, to gain financial footing.
So, when I accrued enough funds, I fired up the engine and explored.
I shifted focus to production and expansion.
I ignited passion into the promise and a brighter tomorrow.

Line 'em up, stack 'em up, rack 'em up, whack 'em up!
That was my motto. I rolled differently when owning the road.
I whipped the wheel and mashed the pedal.
When rolling was the goal, money fueled motion.
I grew wings and glided like an eaglet.

I lived higher from a two-floor townhouse to a three-story duplex.
I ate more and ate better from neighborhood carry-outs
to around-town dining. I drank more, drank better from Thunderbird
and Wild Irish to E&J and Bacardi.
I dressed and clubbed more, dressed and clubbed better from bars
and discos to cabarets and halls.

When material growth was the goal, money was the monitor.


From "dutchies" and "dates" to friends and girlfriends to marriage
and divorce to dutch and dates again. I never forced the cycle
but was ready to spin out, spin-free.
I wanted to live better. I wanted more
than day work, after work and nightlife.


When romance was the goal, money was the prick or petal,
 the thorn or rose.
I desired to pay but couldn't afford the tab.
Had to budget my fun like a drone hovering in the "friend zone."
Yet if she was "into me," after-hours didn't matter.


There was more to learn about the world than Fox News, CNN,
Facebook and YouTube; more to reform than consent decrees;
more to teach than syllabi and curriculums,
and more to educate than pupils in classrooms.


Yet when my goal was finding purpose and peace, money could only
offer links, but perseverance and wisdom could connect the chain.

Even as a golden-ager, I had so much to learn about myself

and what I really wanted out of life. To enjoy

life better, realizing it was never too late

to love life. And never too late to love me—

the wealth of my authentic self and the mess of me

the tossed salad – with pension and social security dressings.


Filled and humbly fed by the Holy Spirit,I await

the direction of more opened doors

and the Commission of Service.

Lord, allow me the platform to voice your will.

For such opportunities, I am thankful.


Money was no issue since I'd never been rich.

So happy to be alive.

Money couldn't disable me– only enable me

during these years––the best of my life.

And I like riches in grace and glory

a whole lot better.

## Sonic Wealth

Thanksgiving. 9:30 p.m. Gilbert's home.
On his couch throne, watching the Vikes and Pats
on the tube. He needs more. His fix
–his dope, dammit!

So he snares his iPhone, scrolls a playlist
and lets Tevin talk a minute; Mariah soar
with emotions, Mary J searches for real love
and Lauryn says the sweetest things.

Can't explain the ripe vibe, the groove
got feelings with no-touch ceilings.
What he is saying is *Dopamine*, really.

Tingling pleasure chemicals in the membrane.
This is what happens when vibes ripen,
stress lessens, moods blend, and memories return.
More than hype, spry spirits rise, smile and fly.

Dammit, it's scientific! Mathematical formulas
of frequencies, rhythms and tempos,
exercises of intellect and tendencies.
Sonic wealth.

The Vikes punch the Pats in the gut.

Just visuals, though.

Cuz he rockin' with Miss Patti.

"Music is My Way of Life."

# Peace Is The Only Place To Stay For Homebodies From The Hood

Who says I don't go anywhere? Well—Nowhere special.
See, I am free as I want to be, where I want
to be when I want and care to be.
I just don't want much.
Now that's contentment
for me. The alignment that affords me– peace.

What makes people think what they do
or where they go is more important?
More meaningful and fun?
They're wrong; they're silly to label me:
a nobody, an oddity, a nerd or a knucklehead.

Enough to make me laugh or snarl, cheer
or growl, wince or wonder.
And you think I'm an idiot? Deprived and devoid
—the novice? Just leave me be–
to sit in my serenity, lounge in my lane
and stand on my stair.
That freedom suits me fine, rooting me.
They should listen to me rather than themselves.

I laugh at storms. Perhaps they should go forth and save themselves.

If I never fly to Florida, cruise to Peru, snorkel in Acapulco

or skydive in Nova Scotia, I'm all right.

Enlighten me, but don't pity this intellectual.

Don't criticize this visionary–if you can't see the universe.

I get it –even if people don't. Their switches don't flip.

I'm built differently, charged with wondrous electricity,

 and damned with delectable creativity.

I get that they don't get me.


How often do I travel? Where and how long?

Nope, never, maybe sometimes, someday.

They talk of coastlines and cuisine, villages

and cottages, theaters, halls and symphonies,

fun and fortune. I get it— Nawlins, Miami, Chicago,

Kansas City and Atlanta—Woo wee!

All treasure troves of travels.

But not really.


I love the lives I lived and the spaces I leased.

Yet when all else ends, no one will be more elated than me.

But until then, I won't straddle the edge or clutch the ledge.

The Alpha in me stays put. I don't run into walls; I climb them.

Perseverance paces me.

Did I say I am a visionary –and used to be a sketch artist?

I recognize, animate and magnify subjects.

I'm root and rocket, lock and socket.

I travel when I want and leave when I want.

Home is a holster, a pocket for talents and works.

If you don't believe me, try me—if you hadn't already.

No matter where you're coming from or going to.

Get it? Now I pray that the Lord gets me.

Keeps me, shows me, and moves me.

Until then, I'm chillin'.

## Haywire Bladder

Two years ago, I could drink like a fish and not sink.
I could handle my liquor. I still can –
if I wanna leap in deep.
Elders say, 'Don't worry, it's only aging. Only the bladder.'
Maybe it is, maybe it ain't. But I'm pissed.

"He drinks drinks" was my label.
Now I'm Harold Hydrant
 cuz I gotta run a lot, puttin' out fires.

When the tinkles tug, I chug; gotta make that sprint!
Sometimes I make it; sometimes I don't
like a jet leakin' on takeoff and sprayin' the strip.

Folks say, 'Give up the booze and drink more water,
eat healthier and count calories.'
Okay, I get it-- but what that gotta do with pissin'?
Don't they know water goes through me too?

But nothing goes through me like Colt 45.
After an hour or so, gotta go-gotta go.
Nuthin hoses the toilet like pony piss.

## Second Coming / Return of the Herd

Take your time, don't wait until the last minute, they advise.

Cool—except at a Ravens game or concert.

You gotta stay alert.

Imagine the fans you gotta scoot and squeeze by in no-size-fit- seats.

Can't get in the mood the way I want, can't get wet. Literally.


Elders say not to second-guess the urges and roll with the surges.

That I should be thankful, blessed to have a pot to piss in.

I'll manage, though, not drinking as much.


Doc says it's natural at 67. Things go haywire.

Prostate gets fatter, muscles get flatter, and we spree-pee.

Yeh, really, this messin' with me.

Like revokin my liquor license—my Consumption Register.


I know God suffers babes and fools

but don't come at me with that alcoholic shit.

I'm no Drunkie Junkie!

I'm a Recreational Relapser.


Sir Pissalot.

## Crowned

Before I heard of Jesus, I was taught
to treat others respectfully and not to lie.
I learned to pray
for eternal goodness and endless mercy.
That was law and order for me, the child.
Straight lines and basic shapes.
Simple, solid blocks.

The rules became smeared terms.
And responses became cracked scales.

Over the years, I've watched
the rowdy cause ruckus for fun. And the enraged
damage and destroy just because.
This made me wonder who registered
 and regulated souls at the gates of hell.

Whenever, wherever the spirit took root,
vibrations radiated.

Souls touched and transformed.
I am a witness.
Not witless.

Even before reading the gospel, I heard it.
I felt the need to know what it was.
Did I need it? The composition, the application?
No academia, no theology.
If I were to own it.

The gospels showed me
hues of sanctity & sin, humility & vanity.
Showed me levels of innocence & guilt.
Showed me degrees of breath & death.

Jesus' ministry taught me.
To learn, follow & lead.
To prophesy. Commit & fulfill.
Persevere and serve.
Taught me Purpose.

He paid the cost
for being
fully human.

# I Never Knew Dirt, And Grass Grew Beneath Rowhouses

I never knew dirt and grass grew beneath rowhouses.
I never saw urban pastures. Now I see
the damn skyline and cityscape. This happens
when neighborhoods are razed.
You escape the fall and return 30 years later.
It's a calling to return to the crime.
I return to garner remains and savor the mess.
I take it all in and sigh without questioning
the dawning of the end.

On East Chase Street, seeds of youth tossed
and swept, blossomed and blended.

In the '60s, I witnessed whites flee, and Jewish
grocers linger for years until they couldn't.
Then black business took its turn in the '70s
before cashing out to Asian profiteers in the '90s.

Second Coming / Return of the Herd

Corner stores, supermarkets, cut-rate bars
and churches, strip malls, clothiers and cleaners,
cleanup blocks and block parties, barbers
and hairdressers, zone schools and blacktops.
Folks congregated on marble steps and cement fences.
"Flashlight" and "Disco Inferno" blasted from windows and
porches.


We handled beef with fists. Few shootings and fewer stabbings.
More vandalism than violence.
Alphas respected street cred—the moving up, moving out. We knew
taking another's life was stupid bitch ass shit, never worth the coffin
or cage.


I look across lots of dirt and grass now
and remember a block, a community lost.


East Chase Street will always be
Undefeated.

# Section Two

*He who has not cultivated his field dies of hunger.*

**-- Ivory Coast proverb**

# Ask The Ancestors

"With his eyes, let him speak!" say African ancestors. They know
we are what we see: How layers and limbs spread;
contours and limbsmatter.  We are what we believe –Products of the
seen and unseen, the imagined and palpable.


If truth is the root, knowledge is the tree;
Perception, its branches; and experiences, the fruits.
Yet the reality is the season—
the settling of senses.


We are what we feel: Tinged visions with fluid optics.
We are eyes that speak our minds to a place
and space, Speak truths
from our very beings.


Ask the ancestors.

## Ol Skool Jazzin

Brutha Saxman, you got me trippin'!
Bald, brown elder eagle, you–in your blue suit—
 Ol skool elegance, you puttin' in that work.
Fingerin' fire! Hurlin' chunks of octaves
in the sphere.
Paintin' the walls red. Hear what I said!
And when you hit them sky notes, I wanna
holla, but I'm too cool to cave.
But the feelin' is felt. Feel me?

So when the rhythm is royal, like Pegasus
takin' flight, the juke is knighted.
And everythin' is alright, alright!

Hey, Brutha Drummerman, you
pepperin' them gold cymbals and thumpin'
backbeats on them, white skins, and blue steel.
Makin' them loop, baba boop,
Makin' them leap, baba boom!
Got my neck poppin' and foot tappin'.
I'm sold on the wickedness of them sticks.
Because you are sneaky with the sizzle.

Brutha Jazzmen, when you gellin',
don't mind me if my cool gives way.
And I start yellin', can't help myself.
Dig it!

# Griot

The duty of every prophet and every priest is to reveal
the purpose and path of man's soul. But the duty of the griot
–and he alone –is to reclaim and resurrect souls of kin.


He protects tribal voices and preserves village vines and branches.
Alone, he sets the course and sounds the chimes for generations.


He attracts circles and commands frontlines.
With his eyes, he encases characters.
With lyrics, he sculpts them.


He recites the rise of the Egyptian Queen of Sheba,
the riches of King Mansa Musa of Mali and the reign
of King Sunni Ali of Songhai.
He delivers folktales of Anansi, the Spider-god.
He portrays colonial invasions and tribal encounters in rhyme.
He narrates Mau Mau's uprisings and the fall of Kampala in psalms.
How the hero wins and where victory resonates.
When the villain is foiled, and why  defeat disgraces.
He is the baton of anthems.

The prophet enters the village and points
to the mountains, where truths are buried,
and tomorrows take root.
His duty is deliverance of the word–
a harvest to fulfill.

The priest shares secrets through ancient rites
that magnify authority and sanctity of the Most High.
Discipline in faith and humility is his duty.

But the griot's duty is to move the word like leaps of lightning.
Through the people, he ignites fires of wisdom and willpower.
A lineage of Alphas rise and rally. Soldiers mount and gallop
to fulfill missions and reap prophecy.
He is  charge of  trumpet and balm of battle.

The prophet tells where, when, and how the fire will burn.
The priest tells how to light, carry the torch.
But the griot brandishes the torch and tells
what it is and why it is lit.

## 13 Ways Of Looking At Artists

### I

Poet

Aural beams across nocturne,

Giving life to soul visions.

### II

Painter

Illusory pigments materialize into spectrums

of space, lines, shapes, and colors.

### III

Dancer

Rhythms sway and pulsate, bounce

and pounce, roar and rave, play.

### IV

Writer

Ageless recorder, golden-eyed re-coder

who feeds thunder to those who starve for truth.

## V

Playwright

Scream in theaters, profanity in courts,

Graffiti on alleys and squares.


## VI

Singer

Quivering throat notes, tinged and

twisted lyrics set free the soul.


## VII

Actor

Unmasked and incarnated, exposed and expressed.

Challenged and transformed, shades

of humanity and breath of immortality.

# VIII

Musician

Fingered-genius, note-painted flesh,

Sanctified sounds and sequences.

# IX

They breathe seeds into blossoms and fruits.

# X

They ignite the spirit with flair and sass, sling and slash.

# XI

They collage the eyes with plumage.

# XII

They mold and sculpt, tease and taunt, defy,

Rebel, dictate.

# XIII

They heed, they relate, they lead, they elevate.

# Drum

Rayford wrestled with his pillow.

He couldn't catch z's. He twisted and turned.

He rolled, leaning toward the bed's edge.

He sat upright in the dark. Sleepy, silent.


Then Rayford discovered the source of concern:

In the distance–a pitter-patter bent his ears.

Messages for him.  He listened, understood

and translated them somehow–like a cobra swaying to the flute.

Grinning, he closed his eyes in surrender.


While swaying to the pit-pat, Rayford thought

 he heard a call.

Or was it a plea?

*Come, my brother. Listen to me.*

*I am Mother Afrika. Come, my son.*


Bemused, he shook his head.

Was he hearing right? What mother?

Not the one who raised him?

So, he listened closer as the drumming grew faint, farther away.

Confused, Rayford did not understand.

He could hear but not see the "we"–in the plea:

the cultural connection or regional relation.

Or will of the womb.


*I want you. I need you. I miss you.*

*I will always love you. Come home, my son.*


Rayford relished the rhythms even as they paused, then halted.

Like Moses parting the Red Sea. What happened? he wondered.
Then Bloop! It was over.

What was that all about? Where's the pit-pat?

Sitting upon his bed, he waited, listening

in the dark. For a drummer.

# Section Three

***Death does not sound a trumpet.***

**--Congolese proverb.**

## Mutt

He was missing for two days.  A dog who never missed an evening.
A street mutt, a day wanderer who always found home.
No new scratches on the front door and no recent barks.

Once spry, he had become quieter, slower.
Old, woofing and wagging less.
He rested in the yard shade more,
hid in corners and under tables more.

Two weeks before, I remembered the end
of his appetite and his wheezing
like a clunky mower, belching gas.
His ribs like harp strings.
The Rat Patrol doesn't care about animals who eat scraps
on ground and grass. They can't care when they litter lye
in alleys and around telephone poles.

"Fluffy dead, he over in the lot by the fence.
 Wanna see?" a witness asked.
Naw, we've been together for 13 years.

He chose his grave like a samurai.

# Farewell, Road Dawg (a poem for Mil 3/14/21)

It's 3 a.m. Valentine's Monday—
way past my snoozeville.  I awakened, kinda.  Turning, tossing over
and over, until eventually getting up and sitting bedside. Wide-eyed
and sleepy, I couldn't shake thoughts of her.

What happened? Something wasn't right.
Hadn't been right for a while.
Something felt so wrong. No return calls.
She just disappeared.

My conscience rattled me, shoved and bullied me
to Google her name. Then, there in the obituary,
I faced her image – a face about five to seven years younger.
A face before the diabetes diagnosis, the finger pinches and needles,
A face before dialysis, weight loss, weakened limbs and wobbles.

Things would be different, she warned
years earlier, for the worse.

*We all gonna die from something.*
*Anyway, When you comin' through, Mr. Man?*
*I need some air.*

## Second Coming / Return of the Herd

Anywhere was better than a two-story jail.
Anything was better than TV, pills, portions and water.


Let's ride, ol' gurl! Nighttime –the right time.


I'm the best entertainment she knows.
And who can DJ a playlist better than me? Noooobody!
As a fan, a groupie—she was easy.


In time of need, words would not apply.
Our pact is unspoken. A bond of hearts
and hands pulls and carries. Links
of moments, chains of hours, gems of occasions.


Reading her obituary made me smile–as I noticed omissions,
the unwritten: the best medicine.
Weekend travels--Ridin and jammin, jammin and talkin
around the city.
Also, runs of chores and errands: groceries
and doctor appointments; and dashes of nightlife:
restaurants, movies and comedy clubs.


We friends, right?
Of course.
With benefits.
That too.

Guess you free as wanna be, Mr. Man.
Yep, so you say. You too, old girl.

So sorry, I didn't know. Wish I had known
before Valentine's Day.
Now I'm clogged with misgivings.
Maybe I need open-heart surgery.

Now that I know, I wonder who said what and who did what
at the memorial service.
Wish I knew what really happened. I'd feel more relieved
and less guilty.

I could imagine her shaking her head, moaning,
'There I go' again, making everything about me.
Even her death.
What else did I need to know? What else mattered? She's gone!

*There are other girls—if they ain't already.*
*And they won't be cheap like me.*
Uh-hmm, would that matter?
*Nope, not really. Long as you treat me right.*
Exactly. Now stop talkin silly.
Be ready when I come through. I gotchu.

I'll be free of her soon enough, she teased.

## Second Coming / Return of the Herd

Not really, my friend. Not really.
Memories are not magic,
though magical, alternate and ascending.

She was free – free of the flesh and matters of this world.
A humble, honorable spirit – returning
to its source, the Creator of All,
in Divine Transmission.

Six weeks before her 77th birthday.
She lived a simple life of plain pleasures:
family, friends and work.

She didn't ask for nor required much—just enough
—to rise, to climb, to stand, and move –forward.
"Flowers die," she would complain, preferring blossoms
of blessings.
Often, I sowed petals her way– 20+ years' worth.
Now that's love to us.

Been a year since her passing—though a month for me
since that fated Valentine's Day Google in 2022.

Now she can get all the air and blessings she needs.

Farewell, Road Dawg.
God loves ya best, Millie.

# A Poem For Linda Joyce

Don't know how I feel. Can't explain

or quite describe. But I can't deny the torrents

of torment. I should know. Dammit, I should know how I feel.

Concussed, conked upside the head, knocked out, numbed?


Words tumble like dice. I twist and count

the spots, trying to decipher a pattern,

a message, a statement, a reply.

All they do is stare, empty but aware.

I scribble down thoughts and unscramble words that don't fit
anywhere and don't say anything much.

Maybe it's me: "box-of-rocks- dumb."

Maybe I'm dead too–just breathing

among the breathing.

Sleep is a gatekeeper of toss-and-turns.


"Call me" is the text. Some phone calls

you embrace like puppies or kittens or anticipate

like fouls in the paint; others you ignore

like telemarketers or block like scammers.

Choosing to answer is the cost, and replying is the currency.

I recognized the caller, but why me?

Good news, I hope, and not the Dreaded One.

It was her nephew, who had called earlier,

so I decided to return the call.


His dearest aunt, one of my dearest friends,

has passed.

Three words, 'thank you' and 'goodbye.'

seemed enough, but not enough,

appropriate but inappropriate.


For hours, in "I'll be damned" darkness,

my thoughts leak without a bruise.

Then, a slow drip from my eye. My nostril moistened.

Dammit! What happened? She was doing so well,

accepting the present circumstances and glowing in hope.

How she coped impressed me.


Yet here I lay, undiagnosed, without a name for my affliction.

Blindsided, de-cleated, erased, deleted?

A pitiful poet, a woeful writer

A clueless clunkhead, am I?

Every day in every way and everywhere, Death calls.

It knocks on some doors and rams others;

it surprises some and shocks others.

Truly ominous. 'Be ye ever ready,'says my pastor.

Prepare as we may, but are we ever truly ready?


Maybe it's me—just being stupid. Death is

the stranger you've seen come and go, recognize,

yet not know by name.

Sure hope my dearly departed feels better than me.

Maybe death means trying

to feel something.

## Letter To Ms. Ethel

Dear Ms. Ethel,                                        July 1, 2022

A bad luck streak convinced my big sister that I needed some
intervention–divine, spiritual, psychic or psychiatric or otherwise.

Wounded, vulnerable, I succumbed to her proposal to "see
somebody."
You asked the questions about my present situation.
You watched me and listened to how I answered.
You read my eyes and spoke of my future.

I listened and wondered if you were legit.
Your process was simple: Closed eyes, held hands, and prayer.
Then you spoke on "things seen"— the good and not-so-good.
You gave options and warnings on my character and characters in
the midst.
No horoscope. No tarot cards.
"What do you really want?" you'd asked.
"This is what I see."
You were always trusting, friendly, gentle
and professional—the axis of our social circle,
consisting of my sister Adina, with associates Amy and Jenine.

For years, your office /thrift shop kept business hours

before the landlord's rent increase and shift in plans forced you out.
From then on, we met at Wendy's.

Later we made appointments at your home, where I picked up "my
protection":

Purple and green oils in capsule bottles.

The purple brought luck. I'd dabbed and rubbed it on my hands and
feet about 3 times a week.

(To make it last longer.) I claimed the space I entered.


Green attracted money. I'd rubbed the oil on my palms and on my
fingertips.

Also, for liquidity and continuity, I smudged corners of my wallet
cash.

Life was good.


In Spring of 2015, I felt something wrong. You began canceling our
appointments. Even if you couldn't make it, you'd arrange a time
for me to pick up my stuff. You didn't answer the door,

and mail piled up.

Then we sat in a cold living room, where you wore a wool hat and
doubled the sweaters. You constantly patted your runny nose with
tissues. Your cold seemed to last a season.

At August's end, your daughter Neva called me and explained why
you were hospitalized at Good Samaritan.
On my visit, I saw the real you, unadorned.
 No dye, but silver streaks, no dentures, and frail.


How elated we were to see each other, to be together again!
Been a minute.
I fussed at you for not telling me how sick or needy you were;
you fussed back. Like old times.
I told you that we could continue to argue issues
when you came home.
But you didn't. Neva called and told me you couldn't.


Tearfully I read 'words of comfort' at your funeral
and witnessed your internment.


I kept your obituary and placed it on my top shelf with pictures
of my beloveds— and four empty oil bottles.
I treasure them like urns.
Like you, they're part of my being.


Farewell, Ms. Ethel
Love ya always,
Gil

# No Wonder

There's only a matter of time until it's over.
The Old Testament prophets warned villagers and royals
of the end.
They pointed to knots and whips in the fields,
swords and spears on the horizon.


But no one listened; no one could see
or understand Death.
Neither could bison and lions huddled
in silent arcs.


I mourned a classmate's passing today.
Her memory sealed in cap and gown.
We were high school seniors in 1973,
and mid-60 schoolers in 2022.


Yet I ponder the sphere of life
and its fit of pieces. Death is
cradle and grave, mercy and curse.

We sway among light and darkness.

In space, we shed colors and hues.

No wonder we mourn.

No wonder we yearn.

For more time.

## 4 For 4

67 years and nothing has killed me yet,
not even the stupid mofo who bolted across
stopped traffic and torpedoed my Town car. POW!
He hobbled away, leaving me wrecked. Someone
from the bus stop came to my aid and asked if
I needed help.

The paramedics on the way to Johns Hopkins asked
if I had insurance, so I got a ride,
heard the siren from the inside for the first time
 and had a CT scan.
I was cleared medically and picked up
by my brother.

That black Lincoln (my "Tonya") was killed
in 2018. I lost another black Lincoln love
(my "Ravyn") in 2019.
Some drunk driver lost control on a two-way street and murdered
her-- right in front of my door.
Then my "Goldie" (a tan Lincoln MKZ) had a car pounce on her
in 2021, and my McKenzie (a black MKZ)
had her backside whacked a month later!

4 vehicles slaughtered– 2 Towns, 2 MKZs– in 30 months.
3 parked and unoccupied.

Blessed, I guess, but I'm paranoid.
Gotta get off these streets.


'And don't buy no more Lincolns,' folks warn,
so I bought a 2018 black Malibu,
and carved space in my backyard for "Mali"
-- instead of buryin' my loves in junk graves.

# To Sir Sidney, With Love

Different—but he looked like me; I mean he

wasn't 7 years old, but if I were around 30,

he'd be me, African dark.


No, he wasn't a pretty boy, not matinee handsome.

He was different—Better.

A magnetic presence on screen.

He sounded different, too –Not street-tough,

but a Clifford Brown on trumpet--a clarion,

tame but taut, resonant as the Caribbean sands.


You didn't mess with him; you listened.

You didn't disturb him; you watched and waited for acknowledgment and acceptance of the declaration.

Even his surname flared: the Frenchy Poy-tee-ay!

Even a 7-year-old knew that!


He wasn't the biggest or worst. Not indestructible

Like #32 Jim Brown or a brash brute like Cassius from Louisville.

 At medium height and build, imposing he wasn't.

But you ain't mess with Sidney!

When he stood up, he stood out like Emperor Jones in an America
where Negroes were often orphaned and fostered, bastardized
and cast aside as laborers, beggars and prisoners.
In theaters, Sidney became the torch, a Paul Robeson for us.
In Hollywood, where cork-greased and white-powder-mouthed
minstrels shuffled and howled, crooned, flipped and hoofed,
Sidney wouldn't; he couldn't!
He meant something different—bigger, deeper;
purposeful and substantial.

Tinseltown didn't stand a chance against the crosswinds of Sidney.
A talented black lead who could command more with a single stare
than others' soliloquies.
In Blackboard Jungle, he laid down the Golden Discipline
to street-tough white kids. What!
I never saw a white teacher or white peers till junior high.

Then came To Sir with Love, a melodrama where a white girl adores
how Sidney teaches poetry. Whether taboo or progressive—what
storylines, what opportunities! And he never let me down.

Then when *In the Heat of the Night* howled

on the scene, and I ain't been right since.

A black detective investigating a murder Down South. Thangs 'bout
to get real. I'm all in!

And the slap back! Yeah, that slap.

Was a Soul Power clap back.

Take that, America! From me and the Diaspora!


Then when Mister Tibbs returned—What!

Who you tellin'!

I'm 67 years old now, and I'm still clappin'.


Even today, I can't just call him "Sidney."

He needs a title…like "North Star" or "Blueprint."

 Perhaps Sir Sidney


With Love

# Give It To Me, Baby
# (for Rick James)

From Canada spun Cyclone Ricky –a renegade head-knocker.

He hit the states when disco ruled. The incessant humping chords,
inane strings and concussive percussions numbed him,

so he ripped the script and tossed the charts.

He couldn't wait—-to fire the old cast and fire up a new squad.

Uh-oh! Rick James–in yo face! Bustin loose

on Motown.


Slick, cocky 'n kinky, yet silky as a doo-whopper and buttery

as a balladeer.

Sex and party animals are the guts of blasphemy

for Bad Boys woofing '80s punk funk.

His band, the Stone City Band, swung sax swagger with synth sauce
and shouted, "Squares are too damn straight!

They all can go to hell!"

Shake it up, roll it around, light it up!

Get down with video vixens!

Yet an eternity of flame and smoke can vanish in a toke or a blast.

And 57-year-old asteroids can crash in cold-blooded winks.

So don't blink without giving him his twinkling sizzle!

Cuz HE'S RICK JAMES, BITCH!

# Section Four

*She is like a road, pretty but crooked.*

**Cameroon proverb**

# Beginnings (Never Should Have)

It never begins where it should have begun:
The glance at the bar.
It never ends where it should have ended:
The moves on the dance floor.
The serenade, the surrender, the anticipation,
the climax: a romance remembered.

A portrait of quaint and quiet was she:
Homespun feline. Her mystique perhaps
caught my attention, attracted me.
Was fragility her trickery? Or my vanity?
Our fate, our destiny–our dilemma–
trapped in a blank.

So, I asked her to dance.
Her carefree stride opened me live.
I'm wondering how she would look, hooked
with my embrace. And how her lips might taste.
Hips like that create their own waves.
They don't need terms, titles or names.

My what-ifs faked, and what-abouts jabbed
while her try-try-agains toyed.
 And I liked it: the tension, the keeping score,
the challenge. At least the way I played.

A late "good night" pressed our lips; they locked,
heart-throttling. We stumbled into the doorway
and collapsed onto the sofa in stiff gyrations.

In time, whatever turned into whenever:
You go, I go; you ready, we ready.
Middle-agers tossed the clock, knocking
and rocking. Like it always was.
But never should have been.

## A Revolutionary Love Poem

before I leave the phone,
say a prayer for me, princess
you're my prayer always.
for your love, I live, I struggle
onward.


be proud of the blessed moment we met, loved
& said, "We do" –we did! That moment,
the hour--we became one power.


do not let my hours, my days & nights spent
from home– empty as curfews, lonesome
as idle time– undermine the purpose
for my being gone.


and poetess, though I cannot spread my wings
among twilight, fly homeward & sleep under that black
magic you conjure, especially for me,
I cannot come home tonight.

yet I shall be with you soon as I can,
for a man cannot be---unless he is one
to his woman – children – people.
we have the power to control our future.

That's the mission: when we control
our riches and resources, we grow.
when we direct our visions, we grind,
we grip, we climb. when we lead, we rise.

though struggles are riptides, we must try
—or die trying, die crying; freedoms denied
–when those lying devils never sleep.

So, princess, before I leave the phone,
remember The Walk & The Way: Live life fully.
Seek, watch & listen, learn. Understand anew.
Regenerate & recycle, and build more.
Rise, stand, command.
Walk the Way of the New World.

till the day I rush into your ever comforting ever waiting arms,

hail the new dawn & watch the sun wake the skies

as soul-love-spirit guides me like stars & sands,

navigates me like camel caravans.

Home.


Keep faith, *imani*, precious.

be strong, potent *juju*.

sweet dreams and peace, *baki na heri*.

## Thank Me Later

I ain't no marriage counselor
or relationship expert.
Hell, I'm a portrait of happiness
and contentment: Divorced, a senior bachelor.
Now I don't mean to spit on anybody's boot,
but before you say, 'I do," lemme holla atcha.

Until you live with her, you don't know.
You two might have dated for months, even years but –
until you live with her day in and day out,night-in night-out,
there is always room for doubts and suspicion.
Even if you're "shacking," you only see what's shown –
readily, intentionally.
The elders say, "If she's good enough to sleep with, live with,
have babies with, then she's good enough to marry– period."

Believe me, I get it. It only takes a second,
a minute to say, "I do."
In the long run, it might even be cheaper.
So, take your time, make sure you really want to.

Now life can be simpler; easier with less psycho-social collateral.
And certainly, cheaper than child support and property liens.

Not to mention the breakup, divorce and alimony. A 50-50 split –if
you are lucky. Feel me?
Whether common law or prenup, you can still get plucked.
So, be ready!

Alright, I know about soulmates and destiny.
And about good times—Like pussy tamin'
a buck or bustin' a bronco. But before you say,
"I do,"– Think!

Maybe a romantic notion or domestic obligation makes you commit,
then a crude gesture or callous comment turns a ripple into a rip.
Before you get all caught up, rung up, bruised and sliced up—
just wait –just think!

Now I ain't got nothin' against marital bliss.
But when that lovin' feeling is gone—it's done,

And home – can be a lonely space of dark days and hollow nights.
You might think I'm wrong but believe me.
It only takes a second, a minute, to say "I do."
Yet it may be more prudent, even cheaper, to reconsider:
Take your time; make sure you're ready.

Thank me later.

## Funny Xxx Things

Funny what u remember at the most peculiar periods

Fuckin' things—like this morning. Dumb ass shit

Like "Are we compatible in bed?"

"U don't know by now?"

Or an anticipatory "Is it good?"

What am I supposed to say?

"Pussy wasn't shit!" Guilty as charged.


Shifting scenes and sex positions, it's on 'n on

Til the break of dawn. Angular 'n perpendicular mounts,

in 'n out routes, straight up 'n down 'n all around.

Like fuckin' range 'n funky things. Straight zoomin' the poom poom.

All round the room—knockin' over things like a goon.

Poppin like a pistol, grindin' to the gristle

–LOL (laughin' out loud) funny shit


Get you goin'—the first thang in the mornin'—Booty call shit. All goody good the same, wet ass. But I beg to differ.

At times some goody-good better than others—

a real mutha. Ain't jokin', I swear!

Second Coming / Return of the Herd

Funny, the kinda shit you remember when
it's dark. Just 'fore the sun peeks out
& my johnson raise up like a sickle.

Us gruntin' like hogs, plain & grump serious
'bout every hump. Cringin' when rollin'
over yo wet plop on my sheet. But smilin'
cuz I know it's your sweet spot.
But never lettin' you know (he he he.)

Funny when u think about suffering heatstroke
on the downstroke. Every designated hitter needs a hit
–a booty to call on—an ass to tear up jus' because!
You know, like, Don't hold back; just get back on track
'n let's go with what ya know!
That "turn back the clock on this ol' cock" shit!
That "Nod yo head, make you giggle" shit!

Just funny what you remember. Hmmm Hmmm Hmmm.
Now what do I do with this appendage? '
N how can I revive this corpse beside me?
Funny, she thinks that her holdin' back
from fuckin' means I can't have my way.
Sends me a message. Ain't that some shit!
Okay, right, just bringin' back dumb-ass memories.

Funny memories, exotic episodes of magic stix gone by.
Wonder what happened to her? She ever wonder 'bout me?

Funny what you think, what you remember in the wee wee hours.
Fuckin' dumb shit, fuckin' good shit
Funny things.

# Section Five

***Evil enters like a needle and spreads like an oak tree. -Ethiopian proverb***

## Blood Shadows

Has the murder rate reached its peak?
The city wants to know.
I don't think so, but nobody really knows.
Though it's epic – an epidemic indeed!
Death towers like pyramids.
Like weeds in the wilderness, they stretch
into days and nights.

Sometimes shadows hover, hide –and drive by,
killing a pregnant mother and her boyfriend
in the front seat of their car in front of their home.
Leaving a baby 2 months premature
to be delivered in critical condition.

Horrors crawl, prowling night and day. Shadows don't
always hide as pedestrians take cover
and peek at glaring sunlight.
Held hostage in the afternoon by 60 rounds
of sneer-and-vomit gunfire on a city corner.

Over and over, across the city, across age, gender, and infirmity,
the curse of shadows devours and buries nightmares in coffins.
Nightly news becomes nuisances of casualties

and localities, yet must-see Reality TV.

Shadows set off alarms for eyes that don't want to see;

for ears that don't want to hear. They wait, watching

as ghastly spirits gather. They shield the cold-blooded and lifeless

and resurrect the dead. While the prey prays

and pour libations of liquor and wine. Tie balloons

and flowers around poles, trees, and wire fences.

As candlelight vigils and benedictions, town meetings
and memorials multiply.

Audacious shadows poison and pervert this city.
They engulf and sin without ceasing.
They aren't the last lords, though.
And "death" and "destruction" aren't the last words
but the latest profanity.

Such is the Karma of the Hunted, where survival is sacred
and dignity is divine.
Yet we can't whimper among the waylay.
We must hold the Cowl of the Hunter at bay
while exposing and eliminating his thrill to kill.
We must neuter Killa Kulture. Yet we must not

lie as rocks in the sea but stand
upon the reefs and anchor the shores.

We must repel the shadows with floods of sustained light.
Let us not run from or dodge the darkness.
We must not shudder but step into the spotlight
–whether sunshine or moon glow. Envelop the energy.
And shine. Bask in the rays of truth, the deliverer from evil.
And transform.

Instead of crying, cringing and cowering from threats
and warnings like "Snitches get stitches," We should respond:
"Fake henchmen get unhinged in the pen."
You identify and nullify gangland nightmares. That's how
you control helter-skelter: cage wild animals.

When waves of evil crash against the shores of civility
and community, we must stand steadfast and battle the enemy.
We must wave and wash away the ashes of trauma and tragedy.

Answer me this: Do shadows bleed? Or do they just cause bleeding?
For sure, they don't stop the bleeding.
And bleeding in the shadows and shadow bleeding ain't living at all.

## Apple Apostle 2

Barefoot Johnny crossed the Midwest, sowing seeds of apples
and the Christian gospel to pioneers and settlers.


God's Angels chose him to be an apostle.
During the year, Barefoot Johnny made rounds and returns,
hoping settlers and farmers had become landowners
and branches of agape love.


50 years later, Barefoot Johnny visited brethren
frontiersmen who had eaten basket-loads before.
For a more lucrative venture, God told him to abort
ripe-red, sweet-tasting glory for hard cider by the barrels.


Though booze sales boomed, the Apple Apostle could not stomach
the acidity of a racist brew and foamy white supremacy
that made congregants reekin' drunk as
rotted fruit and trampled blossoms.


Yet 150 years later stands
Barefoot Johnny's last survivor–
a gnarled apple tree in Savannah, Ohio.

## Evil Has An Adversary

1.

It spills, swells and spreads; Evil

has rhythm. A cavernous cold, a hellish hole.

It pursues and envelopes, topples and buries.

Yes, Evil has an agenda.


2.

Insatiable and omnipresent, Evil is

A twisted clarion for finality and extinction.

A contagion unleashed in real-time,

with sirens screaming and flicking, spinning

and spitting into the black hole.

Perhaps for the last time.


3.

 Evil breathes, seeps and receives:
A US husband stabs his wife dead and gets caught
at the Mexican border.
An elderly woman is stabbed in the church bathroom
before choir practice.
A 13-year-old girl is gunned down at the rec.
A 15-year-old totes an AR-15 to school, killing 3
and wounding 8.
You can smell it in the breeze. Lord, help me
understand such killer cowards and soul-less butchers.
Show me how to disarm and destroy

Evil.
4.
Why is gun violence not a public crisis? Explain
the defense of a murderous culture. Define
the difference between hunt & shoot versus kill & flee.
Who's kidding who? People with arms kill people
without arms.On purpose.
Evil is a wolfpack, a circle of hyenas.


5.
I know my prayers won't stop the killings.
I know better, yet I'm numb but not blind.
Angry, not afraid. Believe me.
I am focused on the journey.
Not to win, but to run, to finish the race.
Evil has an adversary.
Hope waits on the horizon,
as Justice shepherds.
I am the lion and the buffalo.

# Origin Of The Second Sin

It has been witnessed, told and recorded, explained and interpreted,
taught and shared, and yet I wonder:

If Adam and Eve committed the Original Sin

by eating the Apple, did Cain commit the Second?


Where is your brother Abel? God asked.

"Why do you ask? Am I my brother's keeper?

I don't know. Do You not know when, where and why, Yahweh?


I know you killed Abel in the fields.  And for such treason, you will
suffer immensely.

For your treachery, no moment of peace will you find. Nowhere will
you find shelter or refuge.


Cain nodded.

"Yahweh, even if such is so, I will not perish.

You will not rid me so easily. For I am

the Hurler of Stones and Wielder of Fury.

Heavenly One, I was not molded by you.

I was born of Eve, west of Eden,

and swelled by the storm.

I am Cain."

Since your arrogance knows no bounds, you will know not a speck
of love or joy.

I will let no host receive you, no guest relieve you,

and no stranger believe you—I will cast you a pariah.


"Nay, Jehovah. Generations will know me—

and embrace me."


Creature, For your outright defiance, your thirst for blood,

your hunger for power and taste for favor,

I will stamp "Murderer" on your forehead and strike

your lineage  with stripes—so mankind will call you "demon."


"Enough. So be it. This is only the beginning."


And so, it began. Sin unfurled in the world a second time, not led by
Temptation and Disloyalty, not blinded by Ignorance and

Innocence–but struck low by Fratricide and Homicide.

Since Adam, Eve and the apple, newer sins have risen and branched.
Each more deadly and dastardly than the tongue of the snake.

Some untruths are authored, while mysteries run ancient as the soul.

Still, seeds of turmoil scatter; bones and blood splatter throughout
a world out-of-sort, out-of-sync.
Distress and discord take root in our very homes,and erupt
in our streets, cities, and countries worldwide
—all sacrifices–to Cain.

Was he right about future generations
savoring blood and embracing havoc?
Is no corner safe in an Eden ruined?
Is no soul safe during the reign of Cain?

# I Aint from Manuel (for the Emanuel 9)

*A Federal Court Upheld Dylann Roof's Death Sentence After an Appeal.*
*He murdered 9 blacks at Mother Emanuel Church AME.*


Momma,


Forgive me, but I ain't from Manuel AME.
Don't mean to alarm you, but …
That boy was lucky, lucky the cops caught him.
What he has done ain't forgivable. He's lucky
real lucky! Lucky them Charleston cops got him.
Them being hospitable and all, asking if he was alright,
feedin' him a Happy Meal. Guess they have their ways
down here. But I'm not from these parts.
Carolina ain't my home.


I'm from Baltimore. So it ain't goin' down like that,
you know what I am sayin'? Just came to this hearing
to pay respects to Manuel's people
and see what the court gonna do with that boy,
the mass murderer.
See if they gonna get it right this time, Jus sayin'.
Hate crime ain't enuff, and 33 fed charges ain't
weight enuff.

I want him dead, Momma. Forgive me.
But I ain't the one who's unforgivable. I mean,
he's cold-blooded, had to be so dead inside to kill
church folk who welcomed him to Bible study.
Naw, I ain't prayin' for him --and you don't have
to pray from me.
I know what I woulda done; I ain't from Manuel.

Swear I woulda lynched him from that traffic light
he ran through, plugged him 9 times,
then cut him down, wrapped him in Confederate linen
and dumped him in a ditch. Done. Finished.
Government ain't gotta waste no time – jailin'
or executin' him. Justice, Pro bono—hood style.
Naw, No nine life sentences.
Momma, hate like that don't heal—not for him,
not for me.

2015 shoulda been his comeuppance.
It shouldn't have taken two years to sentence him
or four more to uphold his execution.
He's 27 years old now and still breathin'.
You know that ain't right.
Tell me I'm wrong, Momma.
You lived through them hangin's, firin' squads
and gas chambers.
What about the folks who got killed cuz of

outright lyin', brutal lies and scapegoatin'.
They always accusin' some nigga of something
just because.
Naw Ma, ain't no justifyin' him breathin' at all.

He's just lucky the cops caught im.
I would give him that 9 mm discount special.
1 bullet for Pastor Pinckey and each of his 8!
So God ain't gotta forgive me.
Don't look at me that way. Me, Jus evil?
Well, you know. I ain't from Manuel AME.
If there's anyone evil, he's the one.
I'm just sayin' some folks ain't fit to live,
and he's one of them.

I know you do not like to hear talk like this:
No forgiveness, no mercy, no charity, no love.
Nope, Did he feel any remorse? And didn't he
want to leave someone alive to give a firsthand
account of the killings?
Well, I wanna be the first to testify at his execution,
I owe Manuel that much.

Sorry, Momma.

Signed, Noel

## Gulliver & January 6th

A place to rest, he had found. Away from the noise
and nuisance of the city. Yet when he awoke,
he tussled upon the earth like a long-limbed turtle
flipped on its back. Taken hostage.

He couldn't believe that he'd been targeted–
and entangled in a net of spikes and knots.
He faced an arc of tiny angry men
who had climbed one side of his red boot
by a shoestring, scaled the hem of his blue
knickerbockers and marched across his white,
wrinkled shirt. There, they stood
on his chest like scepters.

He, a confused giant, scanned the countryside,
then narrowed on  the fringes of roving, raving,
tiny angry men waving flags, banners and weapons.
They all roared demands.

Meanwhile, in dark chambers, an exiled king
waited.

# Critical History

You don't want your children to learn
about any history other than America the Great.
You envisioned America as the Royal Realm,
not manufactured under crafty construction.

You don't want your children to see
that Kingdom dethroned, that reign ruined.
You want them to see only the pinnacle of "isms":
nationalism and patriotism.
You tell them they live in the greatest nation
in the world because they're the greatest people
in the world. America the Apex, the Ultimate.

Why not let your children learn the truth
about this country's founding?
Your Columbus merely discovered a continent
of Native Indians.
I don't understand your myopic vision and
colorblindness.
You think that only your eyes and only your ears
can determine and decipher.
This is "tunnel vision" and "selective hearing."
 You alone become the judge who appraises and validates.
American History ain't all about you.

We, black folks, too, are American History–
irreplaceable cogs in the making and maintenance
of this country.  And we, too, want to
experience the liberties and freedoms you sing about.
We want to boast, too, and believe what you say
about ideals and principles—but we can't.
No matter how we try, our dreams are drained
and our realities are stark and stagnant.
We want to tell and teach our children that your
schools can properly educate and elevate them.
But we can't.
We must tell our children the truth. We must
protect, prepare, and motivate them to master
challenges that haunt and hinder them.

We know this is critical.
The whole truth must be told. Now tell your children.

Just as slaves fought, just as segregated Union
soldiers fought, and World War regiments fought
abroad and at home, we must fight for our rights.

Like your legendary Patriot Pat said, "Give me

liberty" or death.

Our journeys matter: we are American history too.


Who's gonna write or record our story?

Who's gonna write or record our story, right?

As long as the origins and omegas of moments

and movements are comprehensive and

considerate, I'm with it!


Fact is American History belongs to all its people.

This is what we want our children to know.

No matter the obstacles and snares to detain

or stop our progress.


This is no theory.

American History belongs to everbody here.

## Shit Talk

How do you know if somebody's real or just takin'
shit? Easy– just wait and see. I mean, watch
what they do and listen to what they say.
If they try to convince you by beggin' you to
believe them, they probably lyin'.
If they are too loud and dramatic–look out!
They probably suspect as shit.

Now some guys are smooth with their shit:
they smile and agree with everybody on
everything, explainin' how sensible and practical
they are.
But wait, you'll see sooner than later. The closer
the time comes for proof, the quieter they get,
the less convincing they get. You can't get
confirmation of what they spoke about previously.
It's like their shit all stopped up.
Truth's a plunger.  Be patient; give it time.
Drain or clog. Shit's 'bout to go
down– one way or another.
Lyin' ass shit talkers think everybody is stupid.

Just playback their words, rackem up–chalk
the cue and break. Game on. Watch
where the balls drop. Watch and see what balls
fill pockets of character and integrity.
Truth is real shit.

## Good Cops

In Swahili, they shout kupitisha.
"Ikuaka," cheer the Igbo.
The Hausa clap Godiya.
But young folk in the States pump their fists,
and growl, "Stamp it!"

For the record: I ain't anti-cops. I'm anti-bad cops.
Well, if I'm in danger or under attack
–I'm calling the cops, kupitisha!
Afterwards, I'm hoping –even praying—the good cops come.

I want the Boys in Blue I see on "Cops" TV: concerned,
compassionate and considerate.
The ones who ask, listen and explain– to my understanding.
The ones who make me feel safe
and protected. The ones who sit on the curb
with drunks.  The ones who arrest as  last resort,
who apprehend without assault and battery,
who take you home, call ahead or stay
until help comes.

They ask about your cares and needs. Ikuaka!
I want police who announce their identities, who
keep guns in holsters, who chase, cut off
and corner in pairs, who practice safety first,
and who go by the book.
That's who I'm calling. TV cops. Don't care
if they are city, county or Feds. Godiya!

But I don't want cops I see on news videos. Kupinga!
No, not them, panicky police!
They're the ones who arrive with sirens; they scream a lot
with guns drawn. Don't send them! They don't listen; they don't
look! Kupinga!
They just jump out and rush in.
But when things go awry, they cry "foul & victim."
Suspects and evidence escape;
weapons wander or hide–if they ever existed.

Kupinga! They gonna get somebody killed–maybe
the wrong somebody –and lie about it, cover it up,
underreport it–if report at all.
Believe me: I'm not anti-cop. Ikuaka!
I'm anti-shaky and shady ass cops!

Hey, I want law 'n order –and justice too.
I'm not ignorant, blind, deaf or dumb–
I'm just not anti-bad cop; I'm pro-good cop!
Yet I wonder: Where are all the good cops
when bad cops doing dirty shit? Godiya!


Can't unsee unarmed, unassuming black male and female
drivers dragged from vehicles with children in the backseat.
Can't unsee bullet-shattered windshields and windows. Kupinga!
Is that penalty for resisting arrest or disobeying orders?
When do audacity and arrogance run amok?
Is shooting necessary?
Is murder justified? Does race matter?  Maybe answers are
inevitable–even two-sided: these encounters between enforcers
and innocents.
Is Badge the authority? Is assault & battery
the license?


Instead of "commissioner-speak" and town hall meetings,
how about keeping the oath of upholding the law? Ikuaka
I know enforcement standards exist. I know the relevance
of protocol. I believe "white" police should get "black"
police training.
Because they do it right! Godiya!
They understand  the impact and application
 of the "works." Now that's cultural awareness

and sensibility training to me. Indeed, credibility
and integrity to me. The right kind. Godiya!

I want police from TV.  They console and forgive
DWIs and UIs. They even allow flunkers
of sobriety tests to sleep or walk it off.
Officer Friendly. Kupitisha!

And I want "black cop" law enforcement.
Say what? No such thing?
Why black cops don't kill or injure white folk?
Not a one.
How can you explain why they don't threaten,
or even curse –white folks?
Is this because of policy? Culture? Then why
the drastic disparities in outcomes under similar circumstances?
I want the same treatment extended to me–and black folk.
Trust shouldn't be on trial. Ikuaka!

I'm not talking about thug gangs, armed criminals,
mass shooters, serial killers and terrorists. I
I'm not talking about dangerous fugitives!
I'm ranting about Kupinga! Enemies of law-abiding citizens,
especially unarmed, unassuming black ones.
Explain police brutality, harassment, intimidation,
falsified records, forced confessions,

planting evidence, confiscation, embezzlement,
witness tampering and botched house raids.  Kupinga!

Then enter the ripples of race and currents of culture.
And I pause, gazing at shifting "see-scapes."
Objectivity becomes shaded and nonjudgment-tinged;
oaths muddled and words murky.
Isolated incidences? Kupinga!

Explain the killings of the unarmed and unexpected: blasts
in heads and backs, gunfire in public areas, at traffic stops.
Such candid black and white proofs: Knees on necks,
lengthy headlocks and over-zealous strangles, and on-ground tases.
Kupinga!
Are such arrests legal or even humane?
Does writhing in pain matter? The manner should matter most.
Despite race or creed, task load or the fold.

If the Shield is the code, the highest ethics must be the standard.

The yield must be justice. Godiya!

No exceptions, not just us black folk.

I ain't anti-cop but pro-good cop. And I ain't accepting less.

So when I want justice, I call cops

those with 'black enforcer training.'

because I wanna live.


Kupitisha, Stamp it!

# Liar, Liar, Lips On Fire

My nephew asked me why I hated Donald the Trumpster.

For one thing, my nephew and his boys don't know nothin'

'bout nothin' except their gadgets and PlayStation.

They're just streamin' junkies.

But they dumb as fuck 'bout world affairs and even what's going on

in this country, especially government-wise.

Really, they just don't care about politics –long as they keep cash

in their pockets.

They actually think Trump gonna save them some mean green to

feed their families.

I heard them say as much. They think him cuttin' taxes gonna save

their broke asses.

Are they like makin' $500,000+? Hell no!

See what I mean? Dumb as fuck. They must think they big business-

upper middle class or somethin'.


Rich folkz don't pay taxes but make the govt create loopholes

for them.

That's what the Trumpster talkin 'bout: tax evasion.  It ain't for poor

people and people

of color. See, they are the only ones goin' to jail for not payin'.

Think I'm bullshittin'? Check out the tycoons

and mobsters who pay fines or plead themselves out of prison.

Well, most of em. Feel what I'm sayin?

Shit ain't for you; shit ain't fair. Enough about my knucklehead nephew 'n his yo's.


The Trumpster don't care nuthin 'bout me, you or anybody else— Duh—but himself.

I didn't hate him as much as I couldn't trust him; he just lied too damn much— about everything, especially about himself.

Swear he's a peach-faced Pinocchio.


So again, when I asked knucklehead (who doesn't vote) how the Trumpster got in the White House. He just said, "Votes." Not the type of ballots—electoral college or popular.

Well, American voters didn't put him in; state votes did.

No need to try to explain. Either he got it,

or he didn't.  Just saying.


The Trumpster's victory wasn't as rigged as

a defeat woulda been. But his campaign was jinxed.

The 'ol boy' Republicans didn't like or want him.

He wasn't one of them.

Though cheaters, liars, deceivers, and manipulators were welcomed, he wasn't.

He wasn't a career politician but a crude, shrewd and lewd outsider. And no matter how much he boasted about leading troops

into war, he wasn't ever built to be general of the Oval military.

He was born a silver-spooned brat. Never had to be a team player and consensus builder.

So how is it possible that this guy gonna save the American economy?
With a cemetery of deceased businesses, apparitions of stocks and dustbowls of bankruptcies, wormy corruption and devilish deals.
You sure MAGA ain't short for "maggots"?
Because he sure killin' the global image and rep of the U.S.A.

He's a blowhard that doesn't like nobody who tells him "No" or what to do.
Swear he thinks he's on a reality TV show
firing people. Thank God he only served one term.
And if I can help it, he'll never get back.

Soon as he became Prez, the Trumpster started fuckin' up the Cabinet. First, he hired slick 'n slimy unqualified cronies and GOP "yes" men, then fired them the next month. Chopped their heads off because they told him "No"; they wouldn't legally commit
or risk their image and careers for him.
He wanted to be a Godfather, demanding utmost loyalty, but –
most of all hailed himself.

How can you protect the country from the Commander-in-Chief?
That's what I wanna know.

'Fuck sacred constitutions and divine freedoms,' says the Trumpster.
He got a circle of conspiracy conjurers and oath screeners who quench his thirsting ambitions. Every day he gives the American public a potpourri of faux pas. He's unbelievably

irreverent and incompetent. The only president impeached twice.

He makes misleading, hyperbolic statements and false superlatives about domestic economics and foreign affairs every day.

But mostly about himself.

Check the news and hear a bully and braggart "enlighten" the nation.

But not really.


Though Mr. Law & Order remained eerily silent on police misconduct and brutality on black citizens and particularly protesters, he willingly coded them as socialists, radicals, extremists, looters, anarchists and saboteurs.

Yet again remained eerily silent when radicals, extremists, looters, anarchists and saboteurs attacked the Capitol.

They grave-diggin' their own corpses. And won't even believe it!


What kind of Civil War they talkin' 'bout? Apocalypse and zombies?

Must be the Trumpster Effect. Ain't no way they gonna save America—from and for themselves!

But he continued to irritate and incite his fringe base of insurrectionists while raking in and stacking speaker funds for another round of assaults on constitutional and democratic ideals.

Talkin' 'bout misadventure.


I'm held captive, trying to "wake" yo's
 like my nephew.

## Damn (Re-Up, Nephew)

Damn, looks like you lost everything.

You good, nephew?

Heard the guys talkin'. Sit down, man.

Lemme holla atcha.

Now this world's made of a lotta things. Some pretty,

some pretty ugly.

What I'm sayin' is—-not everythin' is black 'n white.

A lotta of colors out there.

A lotta of gray clouds between the rainbows.

There are good, bad, winners and losers, you know.

Everythin's not on the up 'n up.

Man, you gotta be a chameleon, adapting to circumstances

and changin' with the seasons.

That's whatchu gotta do.


Ever heard of the "Main Ingredient"?

They were a soul music group from the '70s.

They had a hit named "Everybody Plays the Fool."

See what I'm sayin? Ain't nothin' new.

I know things lookin' bleak now, but you can't let nobody

get in yo head; don't let nobody bring you down with their bulls***.


So what, you broke up with yo girl! Shit happens.

Don't lose your head over some tail.

Know what I'm sayin'?

Back in the '80s, I had a girl. She was good to me, especially in bed.
But she wanted too much stuff—a new house, a new car,

new friends.

She wanted stuff more than she wanted me.

She wanted to move on, and I wanted her gone.

You know, like that Tina Turner song "What's Love Gotta Do with
It?"

Oh, now you git it! Like yo man Jay Z says, "99 problems."


So what yo homeys turned on you!

'Let's do this, let's do that–you in, you out.'

They nuthin' but trouble! Fuckem, they bitches anyway.

Told you that before.

Think! You don't have to be a clown

in their circus. Lost yo job—that's a bummer.

So what! You think you the only person lookin' for work.

Look around—there's good work, legal labor if you want it.
Everybody hustlin', you know.

Just don't want you in the streets.  Choices matter, my man.

They can cost aplenty.


I'm retired now—but I ain't always worked.

Comin' outta college, it took more than a year

before I found steady work.  Nothin' to brag about—

but I needed it. And I kept it until I found a better one.
Took a minute.
Like small steps and links in a chain–you gotta keep movin' on
and hookin' things up.
Don't feel sorry for yourself; feel me.
Git yo head outta yo butt!

You gotta minimize your losses. You got a bank account?
Good, you aint one of em young men who hide their money
in the house or yard.
It ain't 'bout trust or loyalty.  What if the house burns down or a
hurricane tears the roof off?
Ain't no need cryin' yo eyes out then!
Ain't nuthin' she or them or a job can do for you then! You need
some kinda record—some official list to keep track of yo loot.
Don't get stupid with yo money.
Do like me—Put it in the bank, credit union— somewhere.
Get a trust fund, insurance policy or tax shelter—someplace.

There's a sucka born every minute—but it ain't gotta be you.
There are good and bad, winners and losers.
The takers and the taken, right?
We are all in it, like gumbo and jambalaya.
We all suck like soup! But don't be swallowed up
like oysters or clams.
Git it together. Re-up 'n rebound, nephew.
Grind and grow.

# He Said, They Heard

*(The Kaepernick Clause)*

Kaepernick said before the NFL game began
that he would sit in the locker room or kneel
on the field when the anthem played.
He would not stand, sing, or pledge.

They said he disrespected the flag and military.
He said the anthem uproar was a distraction from real wrongs.
He said "dead bodies" and "paid leaves" weren't justifiable
for police brutality against unarmed blacks.
And predatory racial injustice.

They only cared about weaponizing their perceptions.
They created a target.

He said he would not surrender. He would be an activist.
So, they booed him, boycotted his games.
They tried to bully Nike too, who wouldn't cut ties,
but extended a lifeline with 'JUST DO IT.'
His platform floated on fan empathy and sailed
on media momentum with Black Lives tides.

Trump labeled kneeling players 'unpatriotic.'

and chided team owners for not firing them.
But NFL execs decided protesters should stay
in the locker room until the anthem played out.

The sports world noticed players with raised fists
who stood or knelt with locked arms.
While others stood with hands over their hearts.
Russian bots 'stirred the pot' with #K.O. Kap,
#Trade Traitors, # DeKapitate Colin.

Opting out of his player contract, he knew he
would be a free agent. Yet finding no takers, he
knew the league blackballed him.
He sued them and won.

He knelt before stars and stripes but didn't sing
or pledge. He stood for victims of police battery.
It was never about the flag, never about
the military. But dialogue for changing
lives, saving lives.
Real talk about pits of poverty, screams of gunfire
and pursuits of peace.

He placed his pigskin at the door. Then stood,
nodded and took a seat at the table.

## Just Asking

America, you taught me to believe in democracy
—government of the people for the people.
To believe I was a citizen of this great country,
but you fooled me, took hold of my hope and faith.
You took advantage of my ignorance, my naivete
(or native stupidity, you might say).

Pardon me; my eyes are sore. I cannot cry
anymore. Cannot turn away anymore,
and I'm not going anywhere.
Say what you will. I'm listening– again.

GOP, you cannot be so delusional to think
2020 presidential was "stolen."
Nah, when you catch a thief, expose a con, or give
a swift boot to a crass demagogue –it's karma.
Like burning rubbish, tidying up and
fumigating.  Good riddance.
So here we are:  Now, you would rather smother
the voices of America. Rather play hide-and-seek
or throw the book away in the name of partisan
politics -- and stall the commander-in-chief's
signature--and us, the US populace.

Must be nice to be in charge, shut down the
legislative operation when it's not to your liking,
but have you no shame?
So how important is my vote?

So, hear me out, America!
You tell me the vote is the heartbeat
of democracy, yet you deny me the right to vote.
Even when you did, you reneged –157 years ago
in 1865. You trumpeted legislation that divided
a nation, rallied a Civil War, and compensated
slaveholders and investors (but not slaves
and descendants). 157 years ago, you allowed
the open vote and reneged 12 years later
in an experiment resulting in dark-skinned
electorates, a Reconstruction not to your liking.
Still, by 1910, the South rose again in a neo-
variant of slavery– Jim Crow. 50 years followed
the black vote was championed as an X-factor,
the de facto deal breaker for change.

I believed in the '60s—the times and movements.
But America, you used my ignorance,  my naivete
(or native stupidity, you might say.) You lied
to me then. And you're doing it now.

I once believed in the ascent of aspirations
in this Land of Liberty.
Now I'm a broken axle of liberties hoped for.
I realize there is also something sinister here,
something haunting in the White House:
The Walking Lies exceptional in their
marketeering of deception. They stagger
to gothic anthems; march, rally, attack.
But when arrested, cry foul and lawyer up.
Blame convenient fears and preconceived illnesses.

Just ask the abolitionists and Ida B
about antilynching laws. Ask Freedom Fighters
and Fannie Lou about voter registration. Ask
the Old South about poll taxes and literacy tests.
Ask the New South why it's déjà vu all over again.
Racism is the lion, roaring day and night.

Ask about redlining, gentrification, and
redistricting. Ask about voting restrictions
trending, like polling machines vanishing
disappearing black and Latino counties
in plain view.

And how many times (4 so far) can the Senate
block Freedoms (to Vote Act and John Lewis.'

Voting Right Advancement)?
[Man, he must be twisting in his grave!]
Ask them why they eliminated 160 days of
absentee voting.
And why 52 new voting restrictions? Especially
Texas, which wants to prosecute poll watchers
for regulating inappropriate behavior.
And Georgia, which wants to criminalize anyone
who gives water to voters standing in long lines.

GOP, just because you lost 2020 doesn't mean you
must hide (or cook) the books in 2021.
You ought to feel ashamed.

I ask: America, how important is my vote–
when you won't even debate voter reform?
When we know there has not been much traction
on the "democratic" terrain since the 1870s and
1960s. So, who's delusional?
No need to storm the Capitol again.
Repeat a lie long enough; it sounds like the truth,
like a groundswell, like grassroots.
Like "breaking news." No wonder there's
confusion, disinformation and misinformation.
I'm not confused anymore—no matter what
the government says or doesn't say –

Second Coming / Return of the Herd

I heard enough.
I know muddle talk when I hear it
and damnation when I see it.

I didn't know my vote had a shelf life of 10, 15
and 25 years. Nobody told me until today.
So, what is the lease on liberty? You didn't tell me
then, but you taught me otherwise.

Senate, tell me why my vote matters. Or why
yours matters more?
Yet here we are on the Senate floor, with stacks
of bills sentenced for death on Capitol Hill.

I'm woke –not sleeping with eyes wide open.
Hearing is receiving; seeing is believing.
I should have listened to Malcolm, Martin,
and Stokely, Baldwin, and Maya too.

Please don't try to gag, blindfold or distract me.
Don't be a sore loser or onery elephant.
Don't keep America hostage.
And don't delay the President's pen.

## Life (Make It Happen)

Life is a pendulum
weighted by sadness and tragedy
buoyed by thrills and miracles. It is
exalted by saints and martyred by sinners.

Ain't no telling what gives in between,
what hangs in the interim:
The bountiful and the fruitless;
the fascinating and mundane.

In Life's presence, words weaken, collapse
and perish.
Yet, at Life's invitation, words gasp and gawk.
Still, it defies expression but disputes description,
and destroys with syllables that cut, stab and kill.

I was ascending to my philosophical peak when
she gave me pause, saying life could be
expressed simply as Trauma, Drama and Shit.

I had to check my footing and regain my balance
with a smile. Yep, life can be
a real mutha. No matter how hard you try
or how much you prepare. Hope can go
haywire, fantasies can crash,
and dreams can dry up. And you don't know,
can't figure out why you keep getting fucked.

I agree with her sarcastic tone and her rascality.
Now I'm back, standing steady, and I continue
my commentary: Imagine if there were no limits
or boundaries, no peaks and pits, deserts or oasis,
roots or blossoms, rocks or weeds, no sun or sea.
Just imagine how devoid this world would be,
a desolate existence of bulk objects and solid
things. Indeed, worse if not for diversity
of tranquility and verve, harmony and vibrations,
muse and music.

She laughed, having never seen such flashes
catch fire.
And really, her life wasn't so bleak, and mine, no
pearl-studded stair.
We only proved that heaven and hell truly
co-exist in this age as visitors, guests, or even
roommates; in fact, they insisted.

I told her about the 'tudes.
Attitude determines altitude and latitude.
And the magnitude of self-esteem rules, fueling,
driving, motivating, inspiring goals and purpose.

Now the world may not cooperate, yet overcoming
hurdles and challenges makes success the
sweetest. We make our own realities; we enhance
or decrease our opportunities for happiness.

'But what about the shit?' she wonders.
'Shit is just stuff you must deal with it anyhow,'
I say. Either you wallow in it, smear or lick it—
your choice.
Not me tho. I'm gonna wipe it off the best I can.
You can accept the stank and stains, but I'm tryin'
to do better, get better. That's living to me.

The better you feel, the better you look.
Uh-huh, we agree. I step over and around shit.
Life is what you make It, what you step in.
So wipe your face, wipe your ass. Watch
your step! Get busy—-and LIVE!

# Out (Coming For Everybody)

**#1**

"Coming out" these days declares hidden desires
–Expressions of homosexual secrets.
"Coming clean" admits the regrettable and unforgivable.
But for me, it's the "coming" and going through
that matters.

I understand that gays struggle and tremble
with guilt. They reek with shame and remorse.
Doubts and confusion collide and explode into shards.
Parental and peer judgment is pulverizing.

But why? Why really? Why should anyone care?
What are they afraid of? One's sexuality
 has no bearing on another's existence.

But understand this: I'm coming out too
–as a straight black man.
My issues aint the same as gays.
Yet I do realize as a people, we've been
discriminated against, marginalized and
ostracized, persecuted and – even brutalized.

However, I do have a problem with some gays.

A big problem. It's called "hypocrisy."
When the once oppressed and tortured become
the oppressor and torturer, THE TYRANT, comes
out and takes the throne.
I'm outing ALL TYRANTS, no matter—
whether they be of government or principalities,
color, gender and sexuality LET ME LIVE!

Don't splash loud colors on my walls, sidewalk
and ceiling.
I didn't ask for it, didn't welcome it.
Never needed it.
It might be beautiful—for you.

Yeah, we might have a lot in common and
–we might not! LEAVE ME BE!
We got issues—but homophobia aint one.
Hear me? Don't try me. Don't play the victim
when you force the issues.  You're the aggressor,
don't try to bully me.

I don't like it. Don't fuck with me.
Do you shit on your people?
Leave me the fuck alone!
America has done enough of that already.

**#2**

I can hear Nina Simone shouting," Uncle Sam, goddam!"

Leave me alone—like you leave the privileged –

the ghosts of Jim Crow: the chauvinists, sexists and colonists.

Leave me be–to protect my way of life—like you

do for police states, the justice system, and populist gunners.

Leave me to pursue the same liberties and

happiness with the same vigor and faith as any

other citizen. If only I could believe it.


Uncle Sammy, I hunger, I thirst, but

your sweet, swollen words choke me.

Your smile makes me nauseous.

Your hand outstretched makes me jittery.

I want to believe, but I can't unsee.

I'm not blind, and I won't be unheard of.

I can't forget what I lived through.

And I can't ignore what I feel: Dammit.

You never believed in me.

## The Lyrical Lion Of Harlem /This Is Why

*Langston Hughes testified before Senator McCarthy and his Senate Subcommittee on Capitol Hill on his association with the Communist Party in 1953.*


My name is Langston Mercer Hughes

of Harlem, New York, by way of St. Louis, Missouri.

I am of African-Irish descent. But that's not all.

I am a world traveler and seafarer called to testify.

Mr. Senator, this is why I am here.


I want truths, too, though I'm certain we won't

see eye to eye or smell nose to nose.

A pie unevenly sliced with portions unequally

given cannot be accepted as fair.


I am a testament and testimony.

Holding the mirror, so America can see

its vanity and venom, its illnesses and illusions.

Yet you question my allegiance.

No place has been unkinder and crueler
than my homeland. Not the Soviets,
nor my mentors, DuBois and Robeson.
I share their quests and pursuits.
Yet I am not a Communist.
We are not the enemy.

As a black man, I feel my manhood is on trial.
But should it be? And not the white man
who has betrayed, enslaved, castigated and castrated?

As men, we demand dignity and respect.
But America has regarded my people as lesser
and inferior. We shouldn't have to ask or beg—
for canes or crutches. This is our issue.

America should be what it proclaims. More than
stars and stripes. More than principles
and mottoes.
Be what she promotes. She must get her act
together. Be a disciple of human and economic
justice. Not a mantra for democracy but a stamp
for human decency.

She thinks we have no choice, no alternatives.
You wonder if I believe what I heard.
If I believe what I see. Should I be trusted? Should you?
Is a torturous 4-century affair trustworthy?

I love this country. But it doesn't love me.
She sees me as a threat to the throne, heir
to the hierarchy.
She doesn't want to give or share love, respect,
or wealth.
Our enemies will not be the same.

Is it no wonder we welcome a new host
and most grateful guests who offer roses
for brotherhood, tulips for equality
and sunflowers for land shares?
Even if Socialism be fantasy or goodwill, we must
explore–and demand more.

There's a Renaissance going on here.
Southern blacks en masse arrived in the North
and Midwest, bringing flairs and flavors
that entice, entertain and enlighten.
Around the globe, things are changing, and I am moved
to gather black core—and mine. Diaspora coal.

I am the Lyrical Lion.

My voice is a weapon of volume and cadence,

empowering hope and humility.

The cargo of my words delivers beauty and pride.

Freedom is rebellious and scandalous.

I am the Laureate of Harlem.


Mr. Senator, therefore, I am here today.

To help make an America for ALL Americans.

# Keep Shining (Too Much Crazy)

"On the streets, they call them "bodies."
Experts call them "genocidal."
"Black on black crime" others label.
Poverty, recession and oppression make "killas,"
chant the activists. And I see, I understand, yet
I don't agree wholeheartedly.  Everybody
got choices. Especially them.

Just because their backgrounds ain't cool
doesn't mean mofos gotta fuck shit up for
everybody else. Just because their shit fucked up
doesn't mean they gotta kill—I mean literally,
Who da fuck they think they are! So, tell me,
wassup with these killings?

Crazy when they don't give a shit about anything
but themselves. They think they can do and say
what they want and dare us to say otherwise–or
else a mofo gonna die! Cold-blooded bastards!

Sure, shit's ugly. But they got dreams and
ambitions too. They got role models like thugs,
gangs, hustlers and heavies.
Black market and dark wide web– I guess they
wanted in. Signed, sealed, delivered. Locked,
loaded, they ready.

Now I ain't no expert, but I know what I've seen
and what I've heard. I stand on it.
Fact is I chose otherwise. Maybe that's why I'm
here today.
Choices in work, education, provision for life and
living. Better choices, legal methods, and civil
responsibilities.

Man, the nightly news broadcast "homicides."
But out in the streets, they call it "Murda."
And no one's immune —not me, not you.
No, I'm not crazy, but I can't shake this
wicked wonder: Wassup with these killings?
Shit's crazy!

It strikes differently when the calamity roosts
at home, B-more city, no less. I know I ain't
marooned on some urban isle where gun-toting
hoodlums rule.

Who unlocked the gates of Hades?
Has there been a jailbreak or early release of
killas —that nobody told me about?
The blood-thirsty have risen, committing the unspeakable.


Too much crazy. To live in a city and hear about
death tolls that rival head counts in Detroit and
Chicago, as well as overseas in Russia,
China, India and Africa. 300+ per year, every
year for 3 decades. Gotta B-more careful!


So, what the fuck! When in doubt –duck!
I'm desensitized and aggravated at the same time. Crazy!
Cops patrol, and politicians campaign against
riptides of evil. What can they do? The 'karma
of kill' flushes them too.
Folks blame gov't when streets aren't safe –for nobody.

Killas are all among us. They're made– born in

menace and mayhem.

They're mercenaries whose code is "Killa Commission":

Cash is king, and the king is cash.

"Money over everything," the Hip-hoppers rant.

They're right.

 And the Ojays *For the Love of Money* still kicks ass.


Got answers or solutions? I'm clueless–but open to suggestions.

Still crazy out here. The killas are getting more brazen,

like stalking zombies and murderous hogs who

worship at the altar of K.A.N.E. (Kill Anything, Not Entitled)

and tag the town with hood hieroglyphics.

Wassup with these mofos?

They brag about hood connex, plots, power plays

and 'finessing' profiteers.


It's mind-boggling, certainly mind-over-matter.

We must be mindful of such spheres of lawlessness.

Be conscientious:  Brave the brazen.

No, I'm not afraid—just concerned -- and conscientious.

We can't live in fear. That's not living at all.

We must be free—to believe

in worth and wealth of a future.

We don't have to spill blood, bust heads

or cut the lines.

We value life and the caliber of humanity.

Bloodshed over disagreements is senseless,
murder over posturing is insanity.
We must care and believe in each other:
Galvanize, serve, build and guard.

We are the reason for the light. Despite the grave-blackness
of those mentally touched, morose evil ass mofos.
Killing and killa cash don't build families, don't
uplift communities or direct gov't. They don't
raise horizons, clear skies or welcome sunrise.
Instead, they rage like feisty flames and ruin
like warring termites.

Guts and glory are the narratives of battle and redemption.
It's a choice thang, a war thang.
Shit's still crazy, but we must remain fearless Beacons
of Perpetual Light. And continue to be
the Culture of Reckoning. We are
the "Wassup" that matters most.

Rise up, Keep shining, y'all.

# **About the Author**

The versatile Lobibah Oji Baraka has been called a "message poet," a "poetic memoirist" and a "tableau poet who creates colloquial vignettes."

His favorite writers are James Baldwin, Malcolm X, Maya Angelou, Dick Gregory, and Ta-Nihesi Coates. His favorite poets are Langston Hughes, William Carlos Williams, Lucille Clifton, Amy Lowell, and Billy Collins.

Baraka enjoys reading and discussing books on topical issues, literature, and arts that reflect and affect African-American society and the Africa Diaspora. Currently, he is completing a volume of memoirs and collecting poems for his third volume of free verse.

A native of Baltimore, Maryland, Lobibah Oji Baraka is a former high school English teacher of 22 years and author of Herd of Tusks, a collection of free verse. He earned a B.A. in English and a Master's in Special Education from Coppin State University. He currently resides in the city.

To say the least, Baraka has a way with words. Read for yourself, then run and tell somebody!

# From the Author

In 2016, I self-published my debut book of poetry, *Herd of Tusks*. The title alluded to the elephant as the mightiest beast in the jungle. My family adopted this behemoth as our symbol.

However, what I desired most was to communicate in varied dimensions with my audience— 'my peeps.' I still do.

## About The Book

This book, ***Second Coming/ Return of the Herd***, is my culmination of a 7-year itch. Second Coming continues the elephant herd theme. The poems dig deeper, wider, and longer than my debut collection. I ruminate over 1960s nostalgia, poet evolution, Christian testimonials and commemorations. Also, I grapple with the impact of crime and criminality as well as the trials and triumphs of being a senior black man living in the Age of Generation XYZs.

# To My Audience

Those whom I read to, complained and explained to, laughed and argued with---you just don't know how much you've stimulated and entertained me over the years. Salute.

My audiences are open-minded, middle-aged, and senior readers who appreciate vignettes of free verse and narrative poetry in eloquent urban vernacular.

This book will also appeal to Christians, social justice activists and spoken word lovers.